The
UNITED
STATES
PRESIDENTS

★ Andrew ★

JOHNSON

Megan M. Gunderson

Big Buddy Books
An Imprint of Abdo Publishing
abdopublishing.com

abdopublishing.com

Published by Abdo Publishing, a division of ABDO, PO Box 398166, Minneapolis, Minnesota 55439.
Copyright © 2017 by Abdo Consulting Group, Inc. International copyrights reserved in all countries. No
part of this book may be reproduced in any form without written permission from the publisher. Big Buddy
Books™ is a trademark and logo of Abdo Publishing.

Printed in the United States of America, North Mankato, Minnesota
062016
092016

THIS BOOK CONTAINS
RECYCLED MATERIALS

Design: Sarah DeYoung, Mighty Media, Inc.
Production: Mighty Media, Inc.
Editor: Liz Salzmann
Cover Photograph: Getty Images
Interior Photographs: Alamy (pp. 11, 29); AP Images (p. 9); Getty Images (pp. 5, 13, 19, 21, 25); Library of
    Congress (pp. 6, 7, 15, 17, 23); National Park Service (p. 6); Picture History (p. 27)

Cataloging-in-Publication Data

Names: Gunderson, Megan M., author.
Title: Andrew Johnson / by Megan M. Gunderson.
Description: Minneapolis, MN : Abdo Publishing, [2017] | Series: United States
    presidents | Includes bibliographical references and index.
Identifiers: LCCN 2015044081 | ISBN 9781680781038 (lib. bdg.) |
    ISBN 9781680775235 (ebook)
Subjects: LCSH: Johnson, Andrew, 1808-1875--Juvenile literature. 2. Presidents-
    -United States--Biography--Juvenile literature. | United States--Politics and
    Government--1865-1869--Juvenile literature.
Classification: DDC 973.8/1092092 [B]--dc23
LC record available at http://lccn.loc.gov/2015044081

Contents

Andrew Johnson

Andrew Johnson was the seventeenth president of the United States. In 1865, Johnson was the vice president when President Abraham Lincoln was killed. He then became president.

In 1868, Johnson became the first president to be **impeached**. The Senate voted on whether he should be removed from office. Johnson remained in office by just one vote. Johnson's presidency wasn't easy. Yet he always fought hard for his beliefs.

Timeline

1808

On December 29, Andrew Johnson was born in Raleigh, North Carolina.

1853

Johnson became governor of Tennessee.

1827

On May 17, Johnson married Eliza McCardle.

1864

Johnson was elected vice president under Abraham Lincoln.

1868

President Johnson was **impeached** by the US House of **Representatives**, but the Senate voted to keep him in office.

1875

Johnson was elected to the US Senate. On July 31, Andrew Johnson died.

1865

President Lincoln died on April 15, and Johnson became the seventeenth US president.

1869

Johnson's presidency ended in March.

Young Andrew

Andrew Johnson was born on December 29, 1808, in Raleigh, North Carolina. When Andrew was three, his father died. As a child, Andrew loved learning. However, his family could not afford to send him to school. So, he became an **apprentice**.

★ FAST FACTS ★

Born: December 20, 1808

Wife: Eliza McCardle (1810–1876)

Children: five

Political Party: Democrat

Age at Inauguration: 56

Years Served: 1865–1869

Vice President: None

Died: July 31, 1875, age 66

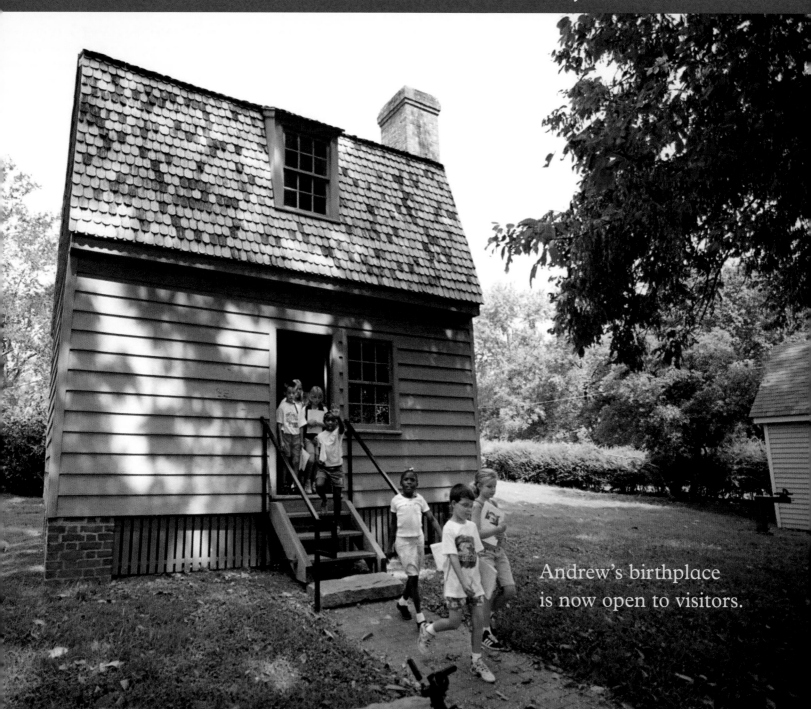

Andrew's birthplace
is now open to visitors.

Tailor's Apprentice

When Andrew was 14, he was **apprenticed** to a **tailor**. The tailor was James J. Selby. When Andrew was 15, he ran away from his job.

Andrew traveled from town to town. He tried to find work as a tailor. But no one wanted to hire a runaway apprentice.

Andrew wanted a new start. So he decided to leave North Carolina. In 1826, he moved to Greeneville, Tennessee.

After Andrew became president, he claimed he could still sew a coat!

Family and Work

In Greeneville, Johnson met Eliza McCardle. They married on May 17, 1827. The Johnsons had five children.

The year he married, Johnson opened his own **tailor** shop. Mrs. Johnson read to her husband while he worked. She helped him improve his reading and writing skills. Johnson also studied the US **Constitution**.

Johnson became a good speaker. He was a leader in the town. Johnson decided to become a **politician**.

Johnson led many political discussions at his tailor shop.

Tennessee Politician

Johnson's first **political** office was on the Greeneville Town Council. He then became mayor of Greeneville. In 1834, Johnson entered the Tennessee House of **Representatives**.

In 1843, Johnson was elected to the US House of Representatives. There, he voted for bills that let some states decide whether to allow slavery.

In 1853, Johnson became governor of Tennessee. He improved the public school system. He was reelected in 1855.

Johnson's excellent public speaking skills helped him succeed in politics.

National Stage

Johnson became a US senator in 1857. At the time, slavery was a major **political** topic. Northerners wanted to end it. But Southerners wanted to keep it. Johnson thought states should have the right to allow slavery.

In November 1860, Abraham Lincoln was elected president. The Southern states feared President Lincoln would try to end slavery. So they formed a new country. It was called the **Confederate States of America**. The states that didn't **secede** were called the Union.

In March 1862, President Lincoln made Johnson the military governor of Tennessee.

The **American Civil War** began on April 12, 1861. Tennessee joined the **Confederacy**. But Johnson didn't want Tennessee to **secede**. He worked to help Tennessee rejoin the Union.

In 1864, President Lincoln ran for reelection. Lincoln chose Johnson to be his vice president. Lincoln and Johnson easily won the election.

On April 9, 1865, the South gave up. The North had won the war. Soon after, President Lincoln was killed. Johnson became president on April 15, 1865.

★ DID YOU KNOW? ★

President Lincoln was shot by an actor named John Wilkes Booth.

Lincoln and Johnson ran against George B. McClellan and George H. Pendleton in 1864.

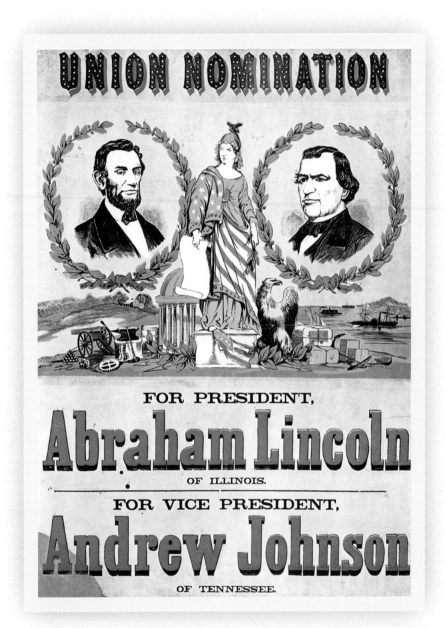

Reconstruction

President Johnson and Congress now had to bring the Southern states back into the Union. This was called **Reconstruction**.

In order to rejoin the Union, the Southern states had to meet certain requirements. These included banning slavery and promising to be faithful to the United States. By December 1865, most Southern states had met the requirements.

However, many Southern leaders now passed laws called black codes. The black codes limited the rights of former slaves.

PRESIDENT JOHNSON'S CABINET

April 15, 1865–March 4, 1869

★ **STATE:** William H. Seward

★ **TREASURY:** Hugh McCulloch

★ **WAR:** Edwin M. Stanton,
John M. Schofield (from June 1, 1868)

★ **NAVY:** Gideon Welles

★ **ATTORNEY GENERAL:** James Speed,
Henry Stanbery (from July 23, 1866),
William M. Evarts (from July 20, 1868)

★ **INTERIOR:** John P. Usher,
James Harlan (from May 15, 1865),
Orville H. Browning (from September 1, 1866)

Many Northern congressmen were against Johnson's **Reconstruction** plans and the black codes. They wanted to secure former slaves' rights. To do this, they wrote laws and made **amendments** to the **Constitution**.

In 1866, Congress passed the **Civil Rights** Act. It said anyone born in the United States was a US citizen. Johnson **vetoed** it. But Congress overturned the veto. The act became law.

Meanwhile, Congress worked to change the Constitution. In 1865, the Thirteenth Amendment had banned slavery. In 1868, the Fourteenth Amendment made all former slaves US citizens. Johnson fought this amendment, but he lost.

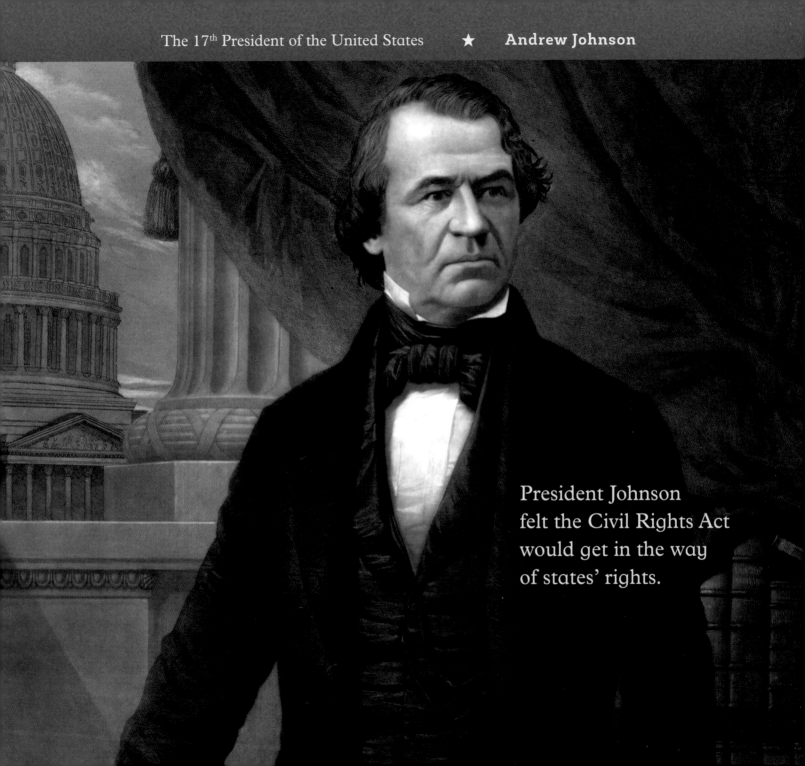

President Johnson felt the Civil Rights Act would get in the way of states' rights.

Impeachment

Republican congressmen feared President Johnson would stop their Reconstruction plans by firing Republican lawmakers. So, Congress passed a new law. It stated that no one could be removed from office unless the Senate agreed.

Johnson tested the law by removing Secretary of War Edwin M. Stanton from office. In doing this, Johnson disobeyed the law. So, the House of Representatives voted to impeach President Johnson.

Edwin M. Stanton served in the cabinets of three presidents. They were James Buchanan, Abraham Lincoln, and Andrew Johnson.

Next, the Senate held a **trial** to decide whether Johnson should remain president. The trial began on March 30, 1868. On May 16, the Senate voted on Johnson's fate. President Johnson won and was able to stay in office.

During his presidency, Johnson oversaw the growth of the nation. In 1867, Nebraska became the thirty-seventh US state. And the United States purchased the land that would become Alaska from Russia.

Still, the **Democratic** Party did not choose Johnson to run for a second term. His presidency ended in March 1869.

The Senate needed 36 votes against Johnson to remove him from office. Thirty-five senators voted against Johnson. He won by just one vote.

Last Six Years

After leaving the White House, Johnson returned home to Tennessee. There, he was happy with his family. Still, he missed **politics**.

So, Johnson ran for Congress. He lost two elections, but he didn't give up. In 1875, Johnson was elected to the US Senate. He began his term on March 4. But he soon became very ill. On July 31, 1875, Andrew Johnson died.

Andrew Johnson had a hard presidency. He faced many problems, yet he kept a lifelong love of the US **Constitution**.

Today,
Johnson's home
in Greeneville,
Tennessee,
is part of the
Andrew Johnson
National
Historic Site.

Office of the President

Branches of Government

The US government has three branches. They are the executive, legislative, and judicial branches. Each branch has some power over the others. This is called a system of checks and balances.

★ **Executive Branch**

The executive branch enforces laws. It is made up of the president, the vice president, and the president's cabinet. The president represents the United States around the world. He or she also signs bills into law and leads the military.

★ **Legislative Branch**

The legislative branch makes laws, maintains the military, and regulates trade. It also has the power to declare war. This branch includes the Senate and the House of Representatives. Together, these two houses form Congress.

★ **Judicial Branch**

The judicial branch interprets laws. It is made up of district courts, courts of appeals, and the Supreme Court. District courts try cases. Sometimes people disagree with a trial's outcome. Then he or she may appeal. If a court of appeals supports the ruling, a person may appeal to the Supreme Court.

Qualifications for Office

To be president, a candidate must be at least 35 years old. The person must be a natural-born US citizen. He or she must also have lived in the United States for at least 14 years.

Electoral College

The US presidential election is an indirect election. Voters from each state choose electors. These electors represent their state in the Electoral College. Each elector has one electoral vote. Electors cast their vote for the candidate with the highest number of votes from people in their state. A candidate must receive the majority of Electoral College votes to win.

Term of Office

Each president may be elected to two four-year terms. The presidential election is held on the Tuesday after the first Monday in November. The president is sworn in on January 20 of the following year. At that time, he or she takes the oath of office.
It states:

> I do solemnly swear (or affirm) that I will faithfully execute the office of President of the United States, and will to the best of my ability, preserve, protect and defend the Constitution of the United States.

Line of Succession

The Presidential Succession Act of 1947 states who becomes president if the president cannot serve. The vice president is first in the line. Next are the Speaker of the House and the President Pro Tempore of the Senate. It may happen that none of these individuals is able to serve. Then the office falls to the president's cabinet members. They would take office in the order in which each department was created:

Secretary of State

Secretary of the Treasury

Secretary of Defense

Attorney General

Secretary of the Interior

Secretary of Agriculture

Secretary of Commerce

Secretary of Labor

Secretary of Health and Human Services

Secretary of Housing and Urban Development

Secretary of Transportation

Secretary of Energy

Secretary of Education

Secretary of Veterans Affairs

Secretary of Homeland Security

Benefits

★ While in office, the president receives a salary. It is $400,000 per year. He or she lives in the White House. The president also has 24-hour Secret Service protection.

★ The president may travel on a Boeing 747 jet. This special jet is called Air Force One. It can hold 70 passengers. It has kitchens, a dining room, sleeping areas, and more. Air Force One can fly halfway around the world before needing to refuel. It can even refuel in flight!

★ When the president travels by car, he or she uses Cadillac One. It is a Cadillac Deville that has been modified. The car has heavy armor and communications systems. The president may even take Cadillac One along when visiting other countries.

★ The president also travels on a helicopter. It is called Marine One. It may also be taken along when the president visits other countries.

★ Sometimes the president needs to get away with family and friends. Camp David is the official presidential retreat. It is located in Maryland. The US Navy maintains the retreat. The US Marine Corps keeps it secure. The camp offers swimming, tennis, golf, and hiking.

★ When the president leaves office, he or she receives lifetime Secret Service protection. He or she also receives a yearly pension of $203,700. The former president also receives money for office space, supplies, and staff.

PRESIDENTS AND THEIR TERMS

PRESIDENT	PARTY	TOOK OFFICE	LEFT OFFICE	TERMS SERVED	VICE PRESIDENT
George Washington	None	April 30, 1789	March 4, 1797	Two	John Adams
John Adams	Federalist	March 4, 1797	March 4, 1801	One	Thomas Jefferson
Thomas Jefferson	Democratic-Republican	March 4, 1801	March 4, 1809	Two	Aaron Burr, George Clinton
James Madison	Democratic-Republican	March 4, 1809	March 4, 1817	Two	George Clinton, Elbridge Gerry
James Monroe	Democratic-Republican	March 4, 1817	March 4, 1825	Two	Daniel D. Tompkins
John Quincy Adams	Democratic-Republican	March 4, 1825	March 4, 1829	One	John C. Calhoun
Andrew Jackson	Democrat	March 4, 1829	March 4, 1837	Two	John C. Calhoun, Martin Van Buren
Martin Van Buren	Democrat	March 4, 1837	March 4, 1841	One	Richard M. Johnson
William H. Harrison	Whig	March 4, 1841	April 4, 1841	Died During First Term	John Tyler
John Tyler	Whig	April 6, 1841	March 4, 1845	Completed Harrison's Term	Office Vacant
James K. Polk	Democrat	March 4, 1845	March 4, 1849	One	George M. Dallas
Zachary Taylor	Whig	March 5, 1849	July 9, 1850	Died During First Term	Millard Fillmore

PRESIDENT	PARTY	TOOK OFFICE	LEFT OFFICE	TERMS SERVED	VICE PRESIDENT
Millard Fillmore	Whig	July 10, 1850	March 4, 1853	Completed Taylor's Term	Office Vacant
Franklin Pierce	Democrat	March 4, 1853	March 4, 1857	One	William R.D. King
James Buchanan	Democrat	March 4, 1857	March 4, 1861	One	John C. Breckinridge
Abraham Lincoln	Republican	March 4, 1861	April 15, 1865	Served One Term, Died During Second Term	Hannibal Hamlin, Andrew Johnson
Andrew Johnson	Democrat	April 15, 1865	March 4, 1869	Completed Lincoln's Second Term	Office Vacant
Ulysses S. Grant	Republican	March 4, 1869	March 4, 1877	Two	Schuyler Colfax, Henry Wilson
Rutherford B. Hayes	Republican	March 3, 1877	March 4, 1881	One	William A. Wheeler
James A. Garfield	Republican	March 4, 1881	September 19, 1881	Died During First Term	Chester Arthur
Chester Arthur	Republican	September 20, 1881	March 4, 1885	Completed Garfield's Term	Office Vacant
Grover Cleveland	Democrat	March 4, 1885	March 4, 1889	One	Thomas A. Hendricks
Benjamin Harrison	Republican	March 4, 1889	March 4, 1893	One	Levi P. Morton
Grover Cleveland	Democrat	March 4, 1893	March 4, 1897	One	Adlai E. Stevenson
William McKinley	Republican	March 4, 1897	September 14, 1901	Served One Term, Died During Second Term	Garret A. Hobart, Theodore Roosevelt

PRESIDENT	PARTY	TOOK OFFICE	LEFT OFFICE	TERMS SERVED	VICE PRESIDENT
Theodore Roosevelt	Republican	September 14, 1901	March 4, 1909	Completed McKinley's Second Term, Served One Term	Office Vacant, Charles Fairbanks
William Taft	Republican	March 4, 1909	March 4, 1913	One	James S. Sherman
Woodrow Wilson	Democrat	March 4, 1913	March 4, 1921	Two	Thomas R. Marshall
Warren G. Harding	Republican	March 4, 1921	August 2, 1923	Died During First Term	Calvin Coolidge
Calvin Coolidge	Republican	August 3, 1923	March 4, 1929	Completed Harding's Term, Served One Term	Office Vacant, Charles Dawes
Herbert Hoover	Republican	March 4, 1929	March 4, 1933	One	Charles Curtis
Franklin D. Roosevelt	Democrat	March 4, 1933	April 12, 1945	Served Three Terms, Died During Fourth Term	John Nance Garner, Henry A. Wallace, Harry S. Truman
Harry S. Truman	Democrat	April 12, 1945	January 20, 1953	Completed Roosevelt's Fourth Term, Served One Term	Office Vacant, Alben Barkley
Dwight D. Eisenhower	Republican	January 20, 1953	January 20, 1961	Two	Richard Nixon
John F. Kennedy	Democrat	January 20, 1961	November 22, 1963	Died During First Term	Lyndon B. Johnson
Lyndon B. Johnson	Democrat	November 22, 1963	January 20, 1969	Completed Kennedy's Term, Served One Term	Office Vacant, Hubert H. Humphrey
Richard Nixon	Republican	January 20, 1969	August 9, 1974	Completed First Term, Resigned During Second Term	Spiro T. Agnew, Gerald Ford

PRESIDENT	PARTY	TOOK OFFICE	LEFT OFFICE	TERMS SERVED	VICE PRESIDENT
Gerald Ford	Republican	August 9, 1974	January 20, 1977	Completed Nixon's Second Term	Nelson A. Rockefeller
Jimmy Carter	Democrat	January 20, 1977	January 20, 1981	One	Walter Mondale
Ronald Reagan	Republican	January 20, 1981	January 20, 1989	Two	George H.W. Bush
George H.W. Bush	Republican	January 20, 1989	January 20, 1993	One	Dan Quayle
Bill Clinton	Democrat	January 20, 1993	January 20, 2001	Two	Al Gore
George W. Bush	Republican	January 20, 2001	January 20, 2009	Two	Dick Cheney
Barack Obama	Democrat	January 20, 2009	January 20, 2017	Two	Joe Biden

"The life of a republic lies certainly in the energy, virtue, and intelligence of its citizens." Andrew Johnson

★ WRITE TO THE PRESIDENT ★

You may write to the president at:
The White House
1600 Pennsylvania Avenue NW
Washington, DC 20500

You may e-mail the president at:
comments@whitehouse.gov

37

Glossary

amendment—a change to a country's or a state's constitution.

American Civil War—the war between the Northern and Southern states from 1861 to 1865.

apprentice (uh-PREHN-tuhs)—a person who learns a trade or a craft from a skilled worker.

civil rights—the rights of a citizen, such as the right to vote or freedom of speech.

Confederate States of America—the group of 11 Southern states that declared independence during the American Civil War. It is also called the Confederacy.

constitution (kahnt-stuh-TOO-shuhn)—the basic laws that govern a country or a state.

Democratic—relating to the Democratic political party. Democrats believe in social change and strong government.

impeach—to charge someone for doing wrong while serving in a public office.

politics—the art or science of government. Something referring to politics is political. A person who is active in politics is a politician.

Reconstruction—the period after the American Civil War when laws were passed to help the Southern states rebuild and return to the Union.

representative—someone chosen in an election to act or speak for the people who voted for him or her.

Republican—a member of the Republican political party.

secede—to officially withdraw from a group or organization.

secretary of war—a member of the president's cabinet who handled the military and national defense.

tailor—a person whose job is to make clothing.

trial—the hearing and judgment of a case in a courtroom or house of Congress.

veto—the right of one member of a decision-making group to stop an action by the group. In the US government, the president can veto bills passed by Congress. But Congress can override the president's veto if two-thirds of its members vote to do so.

★ WEBSITES ★

To learn more about the US Presidents, visit **booklinks.abdopublishing.com**. These links are routinely monitored and updated to provide the most current information available.

Index